Before Girls, grew BreasTs

Enchanted stories from an Irish childhood

BY DYLAN TOWNSEND

1st edition 2010

First published in 2010
by Dylan Townsend
Dublin, Ireland.

www.dylantownsend.com

Cover Design & Typeset by Rani Sheilagh
All rights reserved

ISBN 978-0-9567027-2-2

CONTENTS

Introduction

Part I: Childhood & Family (Pages 8-42)
The Ghost
Mrs. Bloomfields
Snow!
Fancy
Piggy Nose Time
Bowl of cereal
Tree Climbing club
La Stampa Crimbo
BMX
Getting spanked
Friday Night Shower
Sunny Sundays on Sassy
The Treehouse
Estate Chase
Slingshot wars
Halloween Fireball
TV Shows!
Cheech n Chong
Redgey the gardener

Part II: Games (Pages 42-51)

Tip the can
Bicycle Pump action fake
Three and in
Squares
Spit games

Part III: School (Pages 51-64)

Teachers
Talking pen
Copying
Red Renault
Marbles
Johnny

Part IV: Tweens (Pages 64-82)

Sleepovers
Rollerblades
Au Pairs
Golfball Hunting
Truth n Dare
GAA Disco's
Bailey Jumps
Knacker Drinking
Virginity

Dylictionary and Dublinism's (Pages 86)

Introduction

Hiyoo! My name is Dylan and this is a story of stories that I began at the end of my teenage years. When initiating this collection, it was more to steadfast the memories of childhood then to create a book. In the transition towards adulthood, with that sub conscious overhang of getting 'old', I began to write all that I could remember of the 'good old days'. After ten or so stories a theme appeared; Childhoods all over the world, characteristically and emotionally are all the same!

We all to some extent undergoe similar patterns around the fears, problems, solutions, games played and defining moments that bring us into adulthood. These stories are not unique, they are told all over the world in different cultures and while my childhood was in Ireland - and I am grateful for being born in such an amazing land - childhood is full of set mythologies which we all play out in our own circumstances.

I would like to give you an idea of Howth and the surrounding environment. Howth, where the stories take place, is a peninsula which survived on fishing over the last century. When I was a kid it was 'out in the sticks' and it would have been a very distant suburb of Dublin city. Today, Howth is a well to do suburban commuter town. Howth would have been a village in every sense of the word, everybody knew oneanother and there was a definite community ambience.

Gossip was rampant and your misfortune or fabulous moments were on the grapevine before you woke up the next day. The truth is; the Irish love to chat and we will banter about anything really.

Within Howth there are a few landmarks that run through the stories. Deer Park is a huge land acreage surrounding Howth Castle, that is still owned by aristocracy. Deer Park which would have been an ancient oak forest was unfortunately turned into a mediocre golf course in the 1970's.

However, there are still remnants of the forest which are mentioned and this section of forest is still magic. Rhodedendrons flourish here in April/May and the hill turns a purple hue, there are ancient rock formations and the land breathes.

The Harbour in Howth was the village centre for a long time. A pier was built and some of the sea was reclaimed and the Marina added, which brought the centre of the village back towards the hill of Howth. The pier has mangey old fishing boats and thick rusting rope. Its here where you can peer over from the boardwalk to Irelands Eye, a nice sized green island full of seagulls.

The cliff walk in Howth is glorious. The cliffs have a path that skirts the hundred foot drops and the views of Dublin bay are sublime. On the cliffs we have the Bailey jumps which are a configuration of rock jumps that range from 15-45ft. This is the place for summer as a kid in Howth. There is also Jamesons beach which is a pebbled cove with rock pools and lastly there is Red rock which is a set of vast red tinted rocks that became a place to set up illegal raves as we got older.

Thormanby Lawns is the housing estate where I spent most of my childhood. It had everything you need... A football pitch, big gardens, a few sneaky hidden spots and loads of heads to bounce around with. Thormanby is half way up the hill of Howth and is connected to the summit and the village by an old route we called the 'trammers'... these were originally functional tram lines with old electric trains that ran around the hill of Howth but are now dormant.

My family was not your typical run of the mill Irish ensemble. My Irish mother was a prestigous Dublin model during the 60/70's while my English father was a professional tour golfer and my brother became an actor in hollywood. So the house always had an interesting flow of characters and activity.

In terms of the story and naming people. I have substituted names for the characters involved to make sure nobody felt shy being mentioned. The fabricated names are the alternative name that person would have had in another life.

The stories are set thematically into parts between childhood, family, school, games and the tweenies! The themes change with age and the stories begin at the age of five...

Childhood and Family

The Ghost

The house I grew up in was named 'the divot' as my Dad had spent his whole life as a golfer and finally found some land to make his mark on. It was one of the first in Howth and I was told it was 180 years old. There was plenty in there, spirits that is. It was scary and exciting, grandiloquent yet un-hospitable and full of dark somethings. I was fearful of its corridors, musty smells and hidden alcoves and the one area that creeped the most, was the elongated corridor which divided my room and my brothers, which juxtaposed the spare room and a airing closet which was a moist womb cavern that we loved during hide and go-seek.

The Corridor was to be adverted, there was plenty of other places to play anyway. One day I found out why I had an instinctual fear. My best mate Ciaran was over and we were concocting games. We found my sisters ladybird buggy which Chloe carted her dollies in. We chucked the plastic out into the mass of other lifeless-to-become-lifeful dolls and began burning round the house taking turns in the cockpit.

Ciaran Was in the front, I pushing the wheelied wonder along the top floor of the house. We were doing a circuit between the bedrooms and the landing but after a few rounds took a launch towards the corridor... melting down the carpet towards the end and jamming on the brakes just as fast, we stood stricken in feariggurmortus.

A translucent head, drifted up from the floor right in front of the buggy and elevated itself just above us, hovered there and made a gesture in its facade. Well, if we didnt use up our porridge then! we burned back down to our mums and grabbed on for sheer security, shivvering with scarybones.

We went back up an hour later, crawling down the corridor of spirits. The ladybird buggy was lying idle on its side, looking beaten and abondoned, like our minds.

Mrs. Bloomfields

The transition from toddler to toddler plus was not smooth. The realisation that your mother was not at your beck and call was nauseating. Having to be around other kids you didn't know was frightening but what made the whole affair palatable was the amazing old house that playschool was in.

Me and mom would wander through the backside of Howth through the leafy roads until a pair of black wrought iron gates opened into a steep uphill driveway. To the left was a beastly climbing frame made of wood and straight ahead lay a large Noddy esque house built of stone and wood.

The first day I was brought to playschool, I missed mom within thirty minutes and went for a run out the gates and into no mans land. Serious trouble. Found my way half way home and located her, which to my surprise was a problem!

She was not even happy to see me! I got the message then on, this was jail and there was no way out for two hours a day.

The buzz was majestic really. Lots of playtime, making crafts, playing with muck in the garden and claiming "I am king of the castle and you are the dirty rascal!" when you reached the top of the climbing frame. The climbing frame was a technological paradigm shifter. For 1980's Ireland it was top drawer, the thing had levels and stairs, ladders, hoops and perched at the top; a precipice fit for a damsel.

All the boys would scramble out of the house at lunch towards the climbing frame in a heaving mosh of vertical desire. He who climbed fastest was obviously the best, for ever.

I have to admit, I rarely won for the competition was fierce and I had not captured my fear for heights, I suppose that's why we set up the tree climbing club later. Facing fears is the best way to wear them.

Snow!

Frajilistic stuff, white on green ground just makes sense, why do we only get it once a year? Thankfully when we did get that sprinkle, the parents were sound enough to let us be kids... Creeping into their bedroom, darkness sitting in the stillness, "mom, its snowing..." there would be a few moments where the glands would jump into the throat at the idea of not being allowed out to play. " ok, you dont have to go to school." Those words are among other celebrated phrases such as "you can have, I am proud of you and you shouldn't of but I am glad you did." Creaking the door back over, I turn around and would tell Chloe the news, we were free!

Out with the trays for sliding, buckets for sneak attacks and wheelbarrows for snowmen. Clothes were nearly forgotten but by the time all the fun had amounted, mom was worrying enough for our bodies to be turned into Michelin logos. Lombasted with warmth, we headed for the patch where we knew there would be a rhapsody of gas unfolding on the pristine field. No adults, just spontaneity.

We hurt eachother with the snow for a while, when that got sore we united against another part of the estate, usually the bottom estate. After we pemulted them it was time to create a snowball so big that it covered a driveway, if it was a particularly grand ball of angelic, it would stay for days!

The golf course was always a sweet option. Mostly for speed and plenty of untouched snow. Tears were manifold, they were mostly from girls ducts for in the snow the sexes played together when usually, football divided us out. Footballs were still there of course, they were our girlfriends in case we felt lonely. The best hill led you into a reservoir that caused rumbunction and many early go-homes. Life was so simple in the snow: no food, no warmth, no problems.

Fancy

Whenever a collie passes by, I get flashbacks and think "that dog doesnt have the nose of a collie." When you get down to the bare essentials, fancy had a mahussive snozz. It was not useless in its brevity; for it could smell dinner from years away. She was the family dog, that one we all want to find another of when we grow our own family.

By the time I was sprucey enough to play with her, she was past her scrappy days and led a life of pure elegance. She sat, it was a picture. With neck outstretched, paws lying flat , her hind-legs hunkered into the floor as if hand-placed by an indigenous craftworker, she was majesty of all that was ground. To move her from her spot of divinity was, lets say, difficult and enjoyably challenging.

Carefully, you nudged her with your feet and then gave her a couple of digs, then went for a push-rolldogover-mac something happen. She wimpered then, and seeing your insistence thought to herself " if you are gonna get me up I better go the full wack." then it was on! she jumped out of her statue and began burning round the house after you. She skidded along the kitchen floor, burst into the drawers and everyanything, snarling round the corner into the utility room as if she was going to maim you, but in reality she was the most timid but brashfully playful beast and laid down the parameters.

If she barked, you kept going, if she barked loudly you knew it was playing the mischief with her noodle and soon enough you were gonna know about it. So with your mess-bashings and her pretend bites; the level was found and love fell into that bracket of understanding.

As immobility besieged her body(she had been run over three times!) her elegance left her and to keep that overwhelming air of dignity, being 17, she was let go. Not that any of us knew, Dad put her down and four days later, he told us.

Piggy Nose Time

We would get up in the morning, my sister and I, frustrated with tiredness coming off a sugar hangover from the night before. It would be early. No parents and empty bellies brought us kitchen underfoot and the procedure began. Chloe brought the chair, I mounted it and poked the cereal box until it fell into her arms. I could reach the milk and the bowls were found in a drawer beside my perch up top of the counter. Munch munch munch. Only sugarific cereals, 'Coco Pops' and 'Weetoos'. Then the time of cooperation would end.

"piggy nose!!" I would announce as I scrunched her nose with a mauling three fingered death grip that sprouted ferocious girly long nails. She would try and defend, but the grapple on the nostrils was venus nose trap, there would be a brief struggle and then a good cry which woke mom and brought me into a world of trouble. Breakfast was over.

Throughout the day I would catch sneak attacks. In the car home from school, being in differing schools, we would pick her up second and on door slam, a greeting of harassment; boys don't know any better. Flirting was pulling girls hair for gods sake! the degree of beatings inflicted was a flirtometer, 10 digs later, shes mine! Sisters and girls fell into the same 'other' category where piggy nose time only knew the boundary, teachers being the hault clause.

As Chloe got stronger she created her own style of squeeky oink and began to use kicking to a good standard which brought a swifter end to the malicious times. We loved it really, I more than her I suspect.

A Bowl of Cereal

The existence of cereal makes life worth getting up for. Snuggled under the cottons, the lazer beam focus that cereal created was un-equaled in removing that womb of warmth. The walls down the stairs didn't happen and the crunch of coated corn drowned in pure white, made steps become here. Mmmm that kickstart bowl of cornflakes.

The concentration that goes into that first bowl cannot be quantified. 10ml too much milk and you are in for a toughy of a day. Hopping the counter, plucking the largest bowl possible, finding the white were all important, but the extremely conscious measuring of flake, pop or O shaped cereal to milk quota was tantamount to enjoying each unique bite.

Less milk meant more flavour, more milk brought more bites. The gamut had to be epicentre. 'Coco Pops' were everything. Yellow box, monkey boy, a jingle to sing while munching "I'd rather have a bowl...." and an explosion in taste.

But, but. Coco pops were easily spoiled.

The milk had to be 1 exact centimeter from the top layer of puffy chocolatey goodness. Any less, the bowl was dry, any more, you were left with a milk surplus, amateur in anyone's books. I had quite a thing about the end of the milk bottle substance being rancid. One day old or four, that bottom bit was the devils work. If you were left with choco milk at the end of the coco pops, you were entitled to shamidly drink it up, knowing that the next few bowls better be professional or the coco monkey will be calling round on standards inspection.

The boxes were just as important.

Chloe and I would burn down the stairs trying to get the best reading material or biggest boxes so that we could make the best fort around our bowls. Let me explain. For some reason, hiding your cereal from your sibling became the morning sacrament. Five boxes, acting as a cereal fortification would surround your chosen taste vehicle. Drove the parents round the bend. One day we spilled the bowl and all the cereal boxes went gotopplin; that was that. I then began the tradition in other friends houses. I ate out a lot from then on.

'Crunchy nut cornflakes' with banana, 'cornflakes' with raspberry jam, 'Cheerios' with cinnamon, 'start' with honey, 'Raisin wheats' and 'weetabix' with a diabetes type 2 serving of siucra, far to healthy without a dollop of crunchy white sugar.

The list is never ending, either is the love of cereal. Kelloggs are now all made with GM corn and wheat though. Nowadays the mind beats the tooth and cereal boxes are left on shelves.

Tree Climbing Club

Clubs, gangs and being in. That was all that mattered. Probably some young ego trip that also acts as an identity away from being just a kid.

Howth was full of trunks, heights and falls. There was a forest near Deer Park where "the sticks" lay. Here you could climb down one continous tree of branches all the way down the hill to the bottom. It took hours of falls,climbs and pokings to get through it but it was close to flying and there was always band-aid's. I cant find it anymore sadly, maybe we imagined it.

There was always at least 6 of us. Edward, Noel, Will, Donny, Roy and Cormac made up the core club 'members'. The aim was to be king and elevation brought stature. The favourite tree only got climbed on a Sunday.

Getting our weekly pocket money of 20 pence meant we could brum down to the village shops, cram a bag of crisps (meanies), a bar of chocolate(drifter), and a brown bag of apple drops (sticky green sweets) into a plastic transporter that would ritualistically be opened once we had found the support of our tree haven.

The cherry blossoms in the estate were most joyous in spring, twas like climbing into candy floss, once you got there you were stung with wasps which meant the blossoms kept their beauty longer. My garden had the majestic oak tree which we never quite got the better of, the trunk mocking us with its initial jumpchasm restriction and inevitable gaps that would scare the bejaysus out of any young one!

When all the trees in Howth had been peeked out from, hedges became the main attraction. There was one in a neighbouring estate that backed off into an abyss of a twenty foot drop. Hangin out by the bush was fantasmical! you didn't know what was going to happen next. Grouchy people had their bushes attacked often by the club, just to bust chops and risk a little chase. You could make designs out of bush diving, I expect the owners did not see this as art like we did. But sure, perception is always a bitch.

A La Stampa Crimbo

The tree was sublime, an epitome of everything shiny, christmassy and the glory that spits in the face of winter. It shone its best on Christmas Eve, plumped up with piles of presents, most to be given away that very evening. All the colours of crimbo, melanged together into a sparkle, a shimmeration that was dismantled very abruptly.

On the day after Christmas which was renamed La Stampa(a restaurant in the city) when all the family was popping buttons after Christmas dinner, I took my new BMX for a spindizzy around the house. I was doing grand, skidding here, mouthrevving around doors until the glimmer of the tree put me off. It must have shock n awed me with its beauty for I had not seen it for a few hours. My hands lost the break-levers and said BMX went straight into said tree. I was on my own but not for long. The tree crunched me as it timbered and then the tree began to scream for help. The BMX later told me we could fly together...

When the tree would let go of my morning eyes, brekky would call. Then as fast as the turtles 'Donatello' or 'Leonardo' had dispatched of some bad guys on the Telly, we were getting changed for a day of family. Dressed up the ying yang, my sister would be pimped in a festive dress and I would be in jeans, a white shirt and a suede blazer. Chloe had some loverly cute hairdo going on, I parted mine with brylcreem. Mom and Dad always had a scuffle trying to get us out on time but we all knew we were going to be late. Mom looked fabulous without spending anytime on herself and Dad looked himself, which he did very well.

A scramble on the streets for parking. Dad performed the chivalry; letting us out at the door of La Stampa. Sliding into the door, Christmas arrived on every sense. The smell of red carpet, wine and cloves. The sight of heavy coats and weather rushed cheeks. Ear full of buzztacious chatter and tones of 'its finally here," all sweeped through the entrance hall where high society flouted. Kisses, lipstick and hugs, people who say your getting bigger every year and lovely big boxes with bows that tease with the knowledge of having to wait until tomorrow to investigate the contents.

A coke in hand, its all up from here I thought as I clinked glasses with Ciaran. he was there with my Godmother Mairead who was moms best friend. The cousins were all bouncing around and Louis who owns La Stampa would be cruising around amusing everybody with his whipwhit. After such such's and pleasantry's the table would be magically ready inside. Lamping through the hallway, Strange knuttel paintings stared you down with those angular eyejuts and the table was a welcome familiarity. Surrounding the huge table of guests were multiple candlesticks, pre-melted so that the gold encasing was a molten blend of white wax magma. By the end of the night, there would be a few new ones that me and Ciaran would have maxed.

Bread!! this was really my meal, the rest was a side order. By the starter, me and Chloe would have eaten so much butter and bread that food meant nothing but a hindrance until desert came. It took hours! Moments of laughter, climbing under tables, climbing on top of tables, staring at the middle of the table, wrapping on tables with forks professing " why are we waiting, we are suffocating." until we left the table, a shadow of its former decadence. The adults had changed in their demeanor, but we did not get that. Dad always drove home anyway. Stuart would go off somewhere and come back late and be Santa.

Well I think he was Santa. It was when I had been getting a little wised into the shape of things. Doubt had entered, I had heard things in the kitchen. Parents spelling out phrases that I could decipher but would not let them onto. I was getting a snooker table. Stu and Vinni his best mate, were loud and I did the unspeakable and peaked at " Santa clause," which happened to be a wasted Stuart with an elf's hat on him and Vinni, his accessory in a leather jacket. I did not want to believe it. Denial is a place in Egypt and there was next Christmas to think of.

BMX

It was shiny alright. Birthday shiny. Flanked with black BMX bumber stickers and padding, this baby was ready to burn.

The field had the perfect three foot wall for everything. Sitting there became a day long past time; it was part of kerbs(a sporting event of utmost importance clarified later) and also made for a perfect war gauntlet. It was such a friend that after two days on the new BMX, I thought that I should fly over it.

E.T. did it so I was a sure thing. The whole breadth of the field away, I revved the bike with a legspasm and lept into a wheelied sprint across the grass without anything but flight in the noggin. As I got close, there was still no fear. When I hit the wall at full blem, the clatter was such a combustion that I flipped the handlers, carried the path on the other side and melted into the kerb.

It was so Fonze.

Getting Spanked

There was bold and than there was getting spanked. Most of the time I was bold, jigging reactions, but when I maxed it, then I knew what was coming.I would nearly always have to wait and anticipate the spank, hoping that mom forget how far from good the leap was. Dad would spend half the week out of the country playing golf, which kept my ass in dandy form most of the time.

Making a scene in a shop over a toy, spitting, eating 'gobstoppers', pulling hissy fits and strops were part of the spank repertoire. It was a promise and a threat, only the momtone would divide the two. Once I was getting spanked I usually grabbed the reality checkpoint and began harking litanies of sorry and doing nice things for mom like - hugging her leg when she was trying to get stuff done- which was counter productive. Other occasions I knew the gig was up and kept being bad so that I nearly grew horns and took the badtrain to the very ghetto part of spanktown. There was definite levels to the spank.

The day I learned that I didnt have to sit there and take it was quite enlightening. Dad pulled me over his knee but I struggled properly instead of an accepted shuffling of the body, I got free and ran over to mom who gave me no respite but felt pity and I got away with it! I took a few more after that but then came another level altogether, it began to not even hurt! this was glorious... adulthood.

Friday Night Shower

Being a dirty mess was compulsory having a football field for a back yard. Mom never shared the sentiment. Cleaning was an unnecessary shedding of all the good things you had done that week, a waste of time and worst of all there was a huge possibility of getting soap in your eyes.

Yeah I know, pansy. Then came along Johnsons "no more tears" when I was well past my eye fears and well that cooked the goose. The only method was bribery. On Friday we could watch this funny show where contestants got dunked in green goop if they failed to answer some silly questions. Pure genius. People in slime made having a shower and feeling clean just about tolerable.

Our minder at the time was called Anne. She was humurous and did not mind me and Chloe enjoying a good fart which was a comedic occasion any time of the day. "here comes another one just like the other one" I would hark as another burst out. One day I ringed off the catch phrase aimed my arse at Anne, and as she had a much larger bum than me- my little waft parped out- and at the same moment she destroyed the air with a whirlwind and we laughed all Friday night.

Showering is still not as fun but Fridays are better now.

Sunny Sundays on Sassy

The house would be in a scat. Getting us dressed, cleanish, cook delicacies and make a scrillion phonecalls would be moms storm; calm was to follow.

Dad did not care for sailing. Probably because he ignored swimming, fobbing it as simply a method for survival. he would do his best to be excited but usually failed if Golf was on the telly. Mom would have grabbed families all over town for the sunday. The Desmonds one week, Hogans the next or sometimes the Likses or Wilsons.

The only moment of realisation that we were going to Sassy for a sail around Irelands eye was arriving at the dock. Hearing the wind chime off myriad yachts. That the clangjujing brought home. Rushyhurry we were always late. The family who were coming with, staggered round the yaught club telling themselves they should have known to arrive later. Late with a capital LT(Lorna Townsend) Mom would throw sparks and in a second the hour of wait was a fleeting memory as its now time to have fun!

Sassy was loaded, jamskiddled to the nines and there was a buzz in the wind of anticipation. No matter how safe and how good a sailor you are "there are no guarantees." Half way out to the island me and Chloe would get bored. Legs dangling, then Ciaran would get us to play a game and enthral had us back in the moment.

A picnic behind or on the Fred Flintstone shaped island was loverly. Irelands eye was steeped in history as it had one of the Martello towers that dot Dublin which were historically used to watch the seas and send messages around the bay through fire signals. It was said that Diurmuid and Aoife fled Fionn Mccool after a battle on the hill of Tara and lived on Irelands eye for 7 years. After the first year Diurmaid met his assailants and slew those who wanted his blood but six years later many warriors came to Howth and eradicated Diarmuid so that Fionn Mc Cool could bewitch Aoife once again.

We would row onto the island and play chasing in the lush bush. Scraggle round the Martello remnants and then get bitten by crabs on the beach. With Glowy rosebox cheeks, the crew bowled up to the yaght club bar, Me and Chloe got choc n coke. Bounced off the walls and and came up to our parents who were jabberwockyn at the speed of a flapping sail.

We would search the club for gas. Usually wafting into the snooker room but usually looking forward to dinner at Casa Pasta, the only real restaurant in Howth those days. Brimmed bowls full of sloppyjoyjoy eaten surrounded by a boat for a kitchen, the place was pure character. I would moan and call it all "muck" and let those meals go up slack alley. One day I was fishing off Sassy and caught a Pollack, when I got it onto Sassy I broke into tears having killed a fish. The food cycle shared its reality that day.

Sassy could bring out the sassy and the sissy.

The Treehouse

My grandfather, who I called 'poppops' had his ear to the ground. He knew what ran through a 10 year olds mind. His father was called 'the boss' his whole life, of course his son knew the score.

Builders and carpenters began arriving in my garden a week before my birthday. That was enough of a present in itself, men with belts, tools and drills were evocations of enthral. They began working on my favourite climbing tree- the grand oak in the front garden- I was not too happy. I whined like a little bitch until I found out the purpose of the clatteryclang abounding in the garden.

My own frickin house! I did not know what to do... I hung around like a phosphorsence on the shore, lighting up when something became erected and dulled down when I had to go to bed or move away due to danger. The stilts went up first! like an indonesian house keeping out Komodos, the elevation would hault any wandering enemy gang for the height advantage would allow us to hypothetically fire arrows, drop pots of molten oil and heckle with superiority.

It fitted the tree with delight. New wood against ancient living earth. They painted it brown for camouflage, and had a stairs attached an all! There was a porch and then a small hobbit door that was always open. The inside was simple, but fitted 5 or 6 of us younglings.

From here you could climb the tree a mile up, where before, the initial jump was too macho. The tree climbing club was in full force at the time. Picnics, kiss games and wars were   settled in the home. When it rained we sat inside, talking nonsense and making up stories. One winter we spent the whole time collecting balls of mud. There was a shelf inside, that we layed them unto. In spring, hardened, we burst them at eachother, but not all of them, some were still thrung to the shelf last time I looked inside the treehouse.

They cut the old oak back one year and it did not survive the disrespect. The tree eventually molded into the treehouse and the pair began to resemble one of our mudballs.

Estate Chase

After a game of ball in summer and twilight clouding up the goalies eyes, estate chase became the option of choice. The wack of heads playing on the field would all be roped into the game. Ages varying from youngsters like myself, 10 years of age up to older teenagers who would be knacker drinking if they were not playing "man hunt" which was the other name for estate chase. The boundaries were simple. Only inside Thormanby lawns estate, no hiding inside gaffs and climbing trees to hide was a no go. If you were fierce unlucky enough to be on for the first count, you sat by the object of initiation(usually a tree) and were commanded to count 30 off, while the whole estate burned off to find a hiding spot.

From surrounded to emptyville, you were full of buzz and then a
nothing man in search of recruits, for when you found a head you now
gained them as a teammate in the find. The beginning was lonely, but
as you snuck around your crew got bigger and began to plot plans to
find the others. Quarrels would break out among the newly found
block rats, but if you were first on, they usually respected your
leadership as long as you had the moxy to go along with it. Tactics
became the norm as people found devious ways of trickery to decieve
their would be assailants. Throwing your voice or being caught by one
of the heads but bribing them into not letting the original know of his
or her wherabouts was all part of the buzz.

To be the last person unfound was exhilarating. Scampering through
gardens over sheds and into bushes, catching some fella's eye and
mirking back into the shadow of invisible, then leggin it out the garden
at a sprint and all of sudden its on!! fifteen people collectively realise
where you have been hiding, the whiff of awe sifts through the
moment and the race begins. The group would always catch you, but
for moments there is only the idea of being a genius with no plan and
every intention of applying it to brilliance and your friends believing
you are the incarnation of shifty.

Sometimes the game was just a reason to spend time with someone, preferably a girl you dug. I got caught three times one day with Barbera by "fitzer" who had a penchant for abuse but let us both away with it when he felt the love buzz. He was not on, but didn't rat us out which meant we must have come of age that day as usually he would have done something fierce like ambush us. We did not kiss that night but we knew there was a reason we hung around together in bushes.

The first person stung was on next round. It served you right and you knew it. There was plenty of estate. Older kids would break the rules, but that was a right of passage. Your olddom would bring all the benefits that dealing with dead arms and getting spat on through growing up, so that now it was your time to bend the rules. Heads would make noises in certain areas and then run to other vantages to put you off, grokking ingenuity, it was a bit like being blindfolded but with the weapon of ears. If you were it for two hours it sucked the fat one but that only happened if you had enemies in collusion. There was always people who got picked on, it was just about not being pluckable.

Slingshot Wars

Firing things, oh firing things, we all love it. Eventually we took it too far and created guns, but up to that point it must be the endearing idea that you do not have to be close to make something happen. There was water fights with hoses, apple scuffles, spit wars and plane old rock throwing but the slingshot was an evolutionary step. As Ireland was not too up on its kiddie weaponry, whereas in the states you could easily get your hands on a commercial slingshot, we had to create one.

The methodology must have been passed down from another Howth generation, but all I know is that some kid called Graham had a slingshot one day and we all wanted to be as cool as him. Instead of just abusing us with his monopoly on two-meter-combat, he showed us and the wars were induced.

A flat piece of sturdy wood a foot long and a few inches' thick was required as the base for the sling. We would find planks from building sites and each one would make ten. All you needed then was two nails (and later three and four as the proliferation of techniques became necessary during the escalations of war) one on either end of the wood with the round nib of the nail clearly visible so you could hook the elastics around them. Then you would simply stretch the elastic on the nails and fire! Elastics were truly an anomaly, you had 15 one day and none the next.

We could not really ask for more as the rents may find out what we were up to; all war plans must be kept confidential.

At the young age we were, 'Thormanby Lawns' was a big place and the surrounding estates were mysterious yet tangible. They included: Woodcliff Heights, Casana View, the bottom estate of Thormanby Lawns and Balkill at a stretch, which included the trammers(old tram transport lines around Howth) which brought us there. We got on with some of the kids in these areas, but usually saw the locality as a means to fight.

We would BMX out of our homes into a neighbours territory and challenge them to a slingoff. We would return sore. Rocks were eventually plucked and blemmed at one another but then it was scram time. The adrenaline glands were the only winners.

This kid Jerry was a few years older then us but a few bits of sense short, not Jonny no stars or nothing, but he had a disability and always weirded us out a little even though we got along with his younger brother. He had 6 brothers, a real Irish family, house smelling of stew and the mother was great. We wipped Jerry around one day with the slingshots and thought nothing of it. His older brother Dunner thought something of it, found us on a sunny Saturday morning, forced us to tell him where the stash was, and spent an hour breaking every one of our slingshots over his knee.

He was a beast, but so were we.

Halloween Fireball

As the summer days dribbled into an earlier twilight, darkness took fuzzball out of its freeflow and brought about time to contemplate the holiday that was more in our hands than any other. From the beginning of autumn, the Thormanby gang chirped about our grand plans to conjure the best bonfire yet, one that would undoubtedly blaze higher then any local heap of fire. The watershed between school and bedtime gave us a collective two or three hours to scour the perimeter of Thormanby Estate. There was a nettle field, so called due to its abundance of ferocious stingeroos. It must have been a forest that had been cursed for its roots lay under thick grass but no trees grew for us to climb so that we could bounce round the stingbots.

That gathering brought some soggy wood and random items that would flag the fire as decorations. To get the real wood, the kind that is petrol posing as wood and lights so good you knew it never wanted to live; that had to be found out of estate reach.

The Gaelic Football club(GAA club) up the way, had a cornucopia of burn for us. Behind the clubhouse there pulsated a living wood that was not forthcoming in its gifts of dry petrol wood but handed over some spoils if you persevered enough for it to respect you and then award the credit due. It was a 'Lord of the rings' or 'Princess of the bride' forest, that spoke and was spoken about.

We would tell eachother how to get rid of the badgers that attacked you, (by snapping a twig when its got your leg in chomp, it thinks it has broken your leg and should be content and bust off then!) and make up tales of the witch of the wood just for the trembles of darkness that landed around us on those cooling autumn nights. The bounty was hidden back in Thormanby and within a few whiles, the pile grew with our excitement.

Thormanby had two seperate parts, the top part and the 'bottom estate' which had a different set of lads who were mostly nerds to us and never quite got it, whatever IT was. When pumpkins began to get slashed and the sugar cane industry riffled a profit streak, inter-estate battles began. You see, no matter how much we had for the bonfire it was never the size of a house and that just would not do. The 'bottom estate' gave it a go at collecting for there own meagre flicker, and most years we would trundle down out of jurasdiction and skirmish the area with slingshots in belt and plunder their treasure. There was never much resistance for we had numbers and they knew that our bonfire was gonna bring people from all over Howth and that they would be welcome to bop along, as long as they didn't expect friendship.

The eclectic army of sticks, shards, fabrics, cots, nappies, sponges, clothes and newspapers would assemble in the patch right in the middle of the grey tarmac. If it was windy we were ducked, but halloween always came with a soft air. Fireball fights were common, if you could get a 50 shooter you became a firework wielding madyoke, spurning gun shots across the street at your best friend.

Everything told you not to do it and so when one blew up in my hand, I thought it was game over but the thing just left me a rambo scar to tell everyone when school reconvened. When the blaze finally reached its pinnacle the fumes were toxic and standing in the line of smoke was certain damage, but thats what we wanted.

If mischief was not accounted for by a major chase from the piggers then we had failed. As we got older and heads from Howth village came up to the patch it incrimentally increased the chances of being stung by the gardai. We would burst fireworks at there cars and then leg it off, threw apples that we yonked out of kids trick or treat bags and pelted them at the ensuing copper or lobbed bangers under the car while heckling them with such and such harangue. When they finally called backup and got a paddy wagon after ya, it was money! Adrenoline jived the body and survival in the sprint became the reason that bonfire, that emblem for rebellion was created.

Most had their sweets but we had fire inside us.

TV Shows!

'Bosco' brought up this generation. His morals taught us what our parents wanted to but did not have the persuasion power of a television to manifest such ideals. There are Tv gods and he was one of them. He popped out of his box after school and let children across ireland unwind and absorb the message of how to grow up and what to be into. He was really a bit of a freak, he looked like he had chicken pox that never quite became a past and had arms that were knowhere near long enough for his body and box. In ways the anticipation of seeing bosco was better then his speele, the preview screen with a black and white circle turning round as a makeshift clock with the five colours on the side was some pretty fine viewing. This preview screen was what we had before the saturation of advertising filled the seperation between each show.

'The Den' turned Bosco into a dinosaur. The Den puppets were snappy and cutting edge, they knew what we wanted to hear. Latest computer games, simple art projects (not like Blue Peters goofy art presenter) music of the week, lots of craic and above all, insane voices that would attract a young un's attention. Forgetting most of what they said now, I can only recall that they had moxy and that was enough for The Den to GROK

The Den, was host to shows like 'Thundercats!' and 'Teenage mutant hero turtles!' and together this brought more male iconic presence into life then most of the fathers around. 'Heman' also, he had mojo, that sword and those adventures. The 'Thundercats' united and we followed, making the schoolyard into episodes. Which turtle you liked was a reflection of what kind of personality you were, like a childhood version of the beatles for adults or where you sat on the bus as a teen. Together the turtles were cranking, they had a car that any kid would happily live in and slept in the sewer which was pretty rad on all scales. Their weapons were kick ass and they had feelings behind their shells. Bring them back.

'Sesame Street' and fraggle rock were America's mindcompass. They featured in Ireland and it was hard not to love the Cookie Monster or Kermit and his tiffs with miss oinker. They were the childhood soap and fair wacks to Sesame Street in general, it taught things in a fun-yellow-big bird kind of way and mixed in some crazy from fraggle rock just to keep us entertained and off 'riddilin'.

Cheech n Chong

Telly and the Townsends were great friends. Chloe and I would devote a mahussive quantity of time absorbing the outer, with which most of, we could of created within the inner. We played with the blipper anyway, between an array of channels so thick with advertisement goo that there is no wonder my mother had to buy an obscene amounts of toys... telly made us.

When educational slots like Bosco and Sesame street saw their moral high horse crumble into the ditch before the hurdles that no hip kid would attempt, we flicked for a better more out-there option to satisfy the 90's generation kid that we had modelled ourselves on. This brought real life onto the eyeballs, with stoners being of a humurous misunder-yet-everly-over-stood strata of society.

'Cheech n Chong' were pure comedic silliness. The kind of funny that adults had forgotten but stoners kept in their personality trove, ever waiting to be unlocked with the toke of a plant. We watched these men on our screen, outrageous as they were, make sense and find joy in every action that 'normal' people had made mundane. Creating something that was in the moment and huxumurous rather than a chore or some act of repetition. Going to the toilet became an ordeal, making toast, a dramatic series of events that led to toast on fire, nagging neighbours became game components and lawnmowers made the noise of a thousand orchestra's.

One day we saw a movie of theirs. Cheech said he had to go toilet, chong said to make sure not to make a mess. Cheech walks into the dingebox of a bathroom, takes out his instrument still talking to Chong and begins talking a piss in the toilet which is brimming with pooh. Its overflowing with the brown. Halfway through he realises; stops the pile being showered on and croaks to Cheech, saying there is something wrong with the toilet. He decides, to try something else. He smirks at the window with know and throws his lad out that direction. He pisses on the neighbour coming to complain about some such normal problem, gives them a mouthful and telling cheech to stop, we see cheech saying to chong that they should do away with the toilet.

Now that was good watching.

Redgey the Gardener

He would come spiradically to trim our overgrown monster of a garden. It was a combustion of everything; rhubarb, strawberries and raspberries that never really worked, to apple trees that grew over mulchy bushes which melded into the cherry blossom which was the centre piece of it all. Out the front there was the oak tree and a cornucoppia of shrubs designated by the lawn.

It was enough for three gardeners of a young age but instead we had redgey and he had a simple mantra that suited the garden; if its growing too much, chop it.

The definition between flowers,weens, bushes and trees did not really come into the maths of it. My mom had a canary one day when she came home to find the garden in a skip. Redge could not see very well and his glasses looked like they had come from a russian scientists laboratory for people who are clinically blind but would not be let onto the fact. He spent entire days cutting the lawn which was his main port of call. He wore perfect gardeners trousers with check design, grass stains from thirty years previous and a smokers cap which smelt of the proverbial earth from being in so many bushes.

Dad took up the garden when he moved on, who knew how wild a garden could grow!

Games!

Tip The Can

The can was not per se a can, more of an object that could be viewed as a construct for a sturdy icon by which to tip. Cans were trees; there branches and all relatives as well. Climbing cans being the most fun to get to, but then that was really just climbing with a bit of chasing thrown in for good measure. Also declared as cans along times path were umbrellas, skips, hats, cars, doorknobs (precarious) walls and grassy areas.

If boredom ever took the nizzler it was always a group friendly option... Some unfortunate was "on" and was instructed to close his or her eyes against the designated can for a defined period. Cheating at this point was so likely (through peeping) that you ran extra fast away from the to be ensuer. They would finish counting, turn round and feel that empty silence that took you for a brief second having been surrounded by everyone a moment before, only to be filled with the adrenaline pump of "where?"

Jurisdiction became of utmost importance. A 360-degree circumference method was my search of choice, this meant looking like a spare, but meant that you would preempt somebody leggin it for the can; which was the objective of the game. To get there and say "tip the can, I free all" was the aim of any hidden entity, while the look-see had the aim of sliding around like a samurai trying to wurtle into a position where you could see somebody hiding and have room to beat them to the can and howl "tip the can, I see ..... over beside the alley," which would then bring them into a partnership with you to find the rest. As long as you got somebody you were not on next game, which was all that mattered.

The fights over discrepancies about what time somebody shouted "tip the can' and who got there first, were massive. The game was pretty over if it happened as everyone came out for a good banter. Like estate chase if you were last to be caught you were the shit. I played this recently on a Halloween night around the hill of Howth using lampposts as cans, if ever there was a dare; I dare you to arrange a game. Tonight.

Bicycle Pump Action Fake

In the estate where all the heads hung out, there was a gigantic field that acted as a forum for our entire existence. Within it, there was a 50 metre rectangular box of gravel which we un-inspiringly called "the grey". For all daily purposes, this region was redundant but when it came to days on the bikes, this became an arena for combat.

Bikes were our girlfriends. We woke in the morning thinking of where to wander too. We climbed to the top of Howth hill to hurtle back down the "ultimate" which led us sprinting down steep alleyways, bushes, down the dusty trammers, through a few Howth citizenry residences and ended us in Thormanby lawns panting for air and turning the bike around to escalate the hill for another run!

Competitions revolved around the longest skidmark inflictable, the longest "no handler" and the highest front 'wheely'. My favourite comp, and I think the lads felt the same, was played in the patch and usually was our last buzz of the day as it required such skill that you would want to have warmed with all the other trixies.

We would all start by burning around the gravel and try and get eachother out by making the less adept cyclists fall out of the game by making them drop their feet to the floor. There could be up to 20 of us there on the grey. Most only knew the inevitable early knock out was coming their way but for the 5 who were the dodgem bandits, each fallout brought a rush of childhood testosterone and unconscious territorial flagposting.

We would all start by burning around the gravel and try and get eachother out by making the less adept cyclists fall out of the game by making them drop their feet to the floor or falling outside the boundaries of the grey which meant you touched the grass with your wheel/foot, and as there was no referees, this was always a contested judgement.

As numbers dwindled, a huddle formed in some corner of the rectangle. In these acute situations, you would get as close to your opponent and stop, prevent him moving or wheelie up onto his wheels to crash him out. This was a last resort as you were sure to drop a footser as well. You would have three of ya's balanced, knees bent, each peddle half way in its rotation and measured twists of the handle bars which enabled the bike to stand still, like jesus levitating on a bike and then the game was on! You would taunt your enemy and fake crash into him, trying to throw his cool off. Alot of the time we would all topple out together in a combustion of ground shatter, which kicked off the squabble of who fell last and who could claim the right to be called the dodge artist until tommorrows seshh.

A lad came out one day with some new reverse peddle breaking bike and wrecked everyones cheese.

Three and In

Football was it, Arsenal being God. tracksuit, a football, two posts and two mates was an equation to greatness. Knocking over to Noel in the morning always meant I had to wake him, usually forcibly as I was hyperactive and Noel had learned to chill earlier than I. One day I threw a battery at his head, that wasn't cool I later learned and decided I would give him some snooze. Cormac, this younger lad three doors down was always up for a game.

He had a yummy mummy and a gaff full of computer games. We stayed there often; drunk on the illusional characters propelled by our joysticks. Outside we emulated them, playing Fifa (vintage 1994), there was overheads and thirty yard boombizzlers to live up to. Further down the road was the patch and grass for all the estate. Divinely placed were two trees. One curved as if it had grown up on a cliff with a prevailing wind while the other was a boring straight laced stick that was held up by another manufactured piece of wood that eventually had gobbled up the original tree, which gave him a lot more character. When the grass was magically cut on a tuesday by a phantom tractor that worked its way when we did the school thing; it was glory time. Trouble in those days took the form of screeching mothers calling for some insignificant reason such as sleep or food. All three of us had periods of wanting to be the goalie, but usually nobody wanted to get a ball booted at them all game, so there was always disputes. There were methods though, most democratic of course.

If somebody sucked at fuzzball, they would shout "last to hit the floor is in!" but whence we all got to jist, we decided to play peno's for who was in or closest to the post, which was my favourite option. You would go thirty yards back and whoever struck it furthest from the post was in for the game which had negotiated stipulations, such as so many goals and win by two before a change -sub details- which were all too important to the goalie who wants to get out and play ball.

When there was the three of us, we played three goals and the loser went in. If you were on form, you were broken by the end, but thats how the formula worked when you got spent the goalie gloves were thrown your way. The battles were tremendous.

As Cormac was younger- some days you were nice and helped him along- other days you dominated that boy. He got savage eventually and hours were passed in our own world because we had our own tripod reality.

Squares

By pure accidental genius, Fingal County Council created an a game for days that needed filling when the patch was soggy grudgemud. The estate had roads which were planted with mahussive 15 foot by 8 foot slabs of concrete and then slapped by some tar lines, moulding the streets into squares (more rectangular but what the hey) and oh yes the pleasure was fierce!

The original rules were simple; one bounce was allowed in your own territory and once you lamped the ball into anothers, they had to get it out of their's without it going out(the sidepath) or touching the grey twice. Your serve was a throw and had to be fair, you got five lives and a charity doggy life if you were out first.

As we became aware of the surrounding terrain; kerbs, trees, walls and the lines themselves became rulathons. Due to somebody prominent losing a life when it could have possibly been averted, there was an evolution in the laws, long termers formed themselves into squares legacy. All of a sudden, the lines became an extra bounce and a more certain boundary then before was given to those scholarly lines, cross border onslaughts became common but you had to keep at bare mimimum a toe in your own land.

If you skudded the ball in both squares it became a 'dead' which brought some retake to the floor. Kerbs became big players. The trixie player would funk out the other with a kerb reflector as now the kerbs were a free bounce, trees took the same fate and branches gave you time to judge the fall if you didnt have a bounce left.

You could dead ball in others squares by vollying up to there corner and stampering one foot and ball into their square, this was a faux pa of ethical etiquette, it was a life gone at the expense of the respect that would usually be attained at winning through pure trickery. When the finale was ready to battle itself, we doubled up the squares and threw in an extra bounce for good measure. Inventive names were given to the capper who was out first, cabbage life, spoon life, dime bar life and splice life all found themselves a spot in the jestational comrodical abuse.

You were the circle if you won squares.

Spit Games

Sticky putrid games, the height of abuse and the lowest denominator way of going about showing it- with a little gas and skill mashed in. You would be going along having a day and then an altercation began the lungs to extract the flem which would bring about the tears and washing of innumerable sets of clothes.

Grass fights was where it started. Somebody would wiseacre some crack at ya, retaliation was inevitable and the escalation took its own flight from there. Ten kids spitting, the newby's to the game missing and not using any finesse in their strategy. The spitkings would always use the side of the mouth as it used less sound and was unpredictable. while using height as an advantage, you would hop walls and leverage the spit.

A girl in the group was the best. Barbera would have a two inch window from 10 feet and wip you in the nostril. She must have been more dehydrated or something, because her projectiles always stayed together. Skittles were like tribal wears to the spitking, t-shirts being turned into rainbow quagmires. Tears were not uncommon with the humiliation that could come with a barrage of spittle and if the gang teamed up on your ass. The sugary spit fights were the worst. On the high from a packet of E colourings, the spit agglutinated into a toxic substance that could only be described as war goup.

I punched a girl one day, it was her; the spitqueen. She never bust my balls to much after that and I never hit a girl again
(accept the sister but she's not a girl.)

School

Teachers

Everyone thinks their primary school was the best. In many ways
everyone is right. It was how school should be; no responsibility, fun
taking prominence over academia and teachers being as much kids as
the pupils. There was only one shock in the whole of primary
education that stank of academia and that was when we moved from
senior infants to 1st class which corresponded with the class being let
off at 3 o clock instead of the pleasurely 12.30.

The principal had all the hallmarks of a pig in a suit. His personality
was snorty, his shuffles were made as if he had troughs and his face
was shaped like an oinker. The only thing that made him human was
his compassion for a kid in trouble. You would dread sitting outside
McGinty's office but once you got in there he was as reasonable as
grass growing for cows.

Our first teacher who's name is un-recallable (you only remember the
mean ones sadly) was a complete angel. She hugged each member of
the class at the end of the day, brought in sweets, let our creativity
flout and gave us stars on our copy books for being good. The day
began with play which meant the boys played with blocs and the girls
with dolls. She would arrive in and ask us all how we are, did we have
anything to say and what would we like to do today. We drew, read
stories and painted until the chocolate and strawberry milk lady came
in and gave us cartons before our nap.

Waking, we went outside, played some simple games and then coming back in, sat and talked about what we had learned until our mothers plucked us.

When that new lengthened day was introduced we were in Mr Keegans class. He had a rep for hanging a kid on some coat hangers but I never could see it, he was a dude and that was that. He taught us pottery and maths, how to cross the road and the danger (and merits) of fire. Sweet days became the norm under him, where everyone wore there own wears, bought themselves a 6 hour sugar fix and everybody lost it in the classroom. Next came Mr O'Reilly who brought great fear. He was a stickler for Geography and made learning the islands and mountains around Ireland as of the utmost importance. I still frickin know them. A whole weekend spent fretting over a Monday morning grilling was horrific. He stood the class up "you can sit down when you have answered three questions right." you know who was left standing, facing a 100 lines for not learning(or not learning to overcome my fears for an elder) my homework. He looked like a rat and that was him.

Cumisky! now this teacher took it to the bridge. According to all memory he was a nerd who got bullied in school and wanted to come back and take it out on the next generation. By his class I was quite popular and also stupid but witty enough to bust his chops... He tried adopting all sorts of teacher manual methodology to try and calm the 'problem child' but it only raised my game

I asked questions that wrecked his noodle, silly ones with no real answer, in reality, I was probably just dumb trying to cover it but either way it worked a treat. He stayed one year and then went to Kenya to be charitable. Hope he's well now because he was one patient teacher.

By 5th class we were handed a freaker. Mr Doyle ran the choir and had a catch phrase for teaching it "perfect practice makes perfection." The three p's sucked as did his outfit that had not been changed since the 1970's. He is still wearing the same jumper. He taught with an iron fist, lambasting silence over the classroom for large parts of the day. He was the head ant and we were chairman mao's unwilling subjects.

The next and final year was whimsy. McInerny was a sound man and nobody got the best of him. He had integrity and kids no matter what age could respect that. With a face that resembled a rat he was as shrewd as one, never letting nothing slip. He smelled your fear and snuffeted out any kind of cheek. He ran the sprint team which consisted of myself as I was as very thin and was called the Ethiopian back in those days and had no muscle or bones to weigh me down. We ran in Santry and it was all very serious but if you impressed McInerny you were golden.

He let us have water fights during the summer, we did not have to drink our milk under him and he got us ready for the vulnerability of secondary school by kicking the confidence out of our cocky gestures.

He was school.

The Talking Pen

Going to America definitely had its perks in those days. Coming back
with a load of gimmicks was not only amusing but turned the
classroom into a playground. Arriving back from Boston with a mega
super soaker water gun, a new football and a pen that was more of a
friend then an instrument; was quite a landing. The first two
substances made burrows into my world early, it being summer, but
the pen had to wait until September to make its true inroads.

It had three buttons, each spotted with a symbol; one being green the
others yellow and red. The magic presser was red, like every button
should be, it was illuminated by revolution- at least with this red one I
could actually press it! The end of everything did not occur with such
an indentation, more a humorous recording of aural ambience in the
vicinity.

Working my way around its parameters for a few weeks, I made fart
noises and pressed the yellow to regurge the splurge. Made barking
noises for my dog fancy to trip over on and created other
rambunctions under the guise of blackmail by recording my sisters
rants about somewhobody or recorded people swearing which was a
no-no back then. In other words, I became a snitchy journalist without
the internet to properly execute the operation of getting others in
trouble.

It was invincible, I must have really thought so anyway. Daring, I brought it into the classroom and placed in my pencil case, acclimatised it to a whole new world of fun and trixy. Cumisky started losing his head at me a lot that year, I had learned a little humour that summer and transferred his boxes to circles. Sinead and Catriona sat with me at the back of the class, taunting me to go further. I saw it coming and pressed the red... a rant of abuse so calculated and humiliating followed that would cloud Cumisky for months.

At pivotal silences, one of the girls would yonk the pen and squirt the yellow all over the airwaves. In short three or four seconds blurts, this tirade would jump into the room, bringing a nice rosy face to Cumisky. Genius Americans!

Copying

Being a dumb kid is either a call for prejudice or popularity depending on which postcode you inhabit in Dublin. In Sutton there was no chance of justifying my lack of smarts. Each day was a struggle, but sport made up for the burden of class. There were ways around the silly's.

Not getting exercises done on time brought on a duo-policy of justification for the slow finishing of set remedial tasks. Going to the toilet meant that I could claim lack of time spent on the exercise- and this walk to the bathroom- brought ample peeping time to glance into an array of copybooks as I drifted to the bathroom for the 7th time that morning. Back at my seat I filled up with happiness, I knew the answers and the fact that I was copying eradicated itself, much like I would say a klipto finds content in their new found treasure without the guilty conscience. This worked way to well and went on for years. The teachers probably knew but felt pity. Then Mr O'Reilly had to bunch it up.

He twigged me, probably for a week of spyvision, as when he began the public humiliation I had copied an entire page from a clever girl called Aileen across the way. He asked me to stand up and wax lyrical on my answers, with glee I did so- having been on a good run lately- sitting beside the clever heads. Reeling away, the ticks and affirmations of well done came from the teacher; but from a different place in his voice. Then he laid it down with a call on Aileen to recite her answers.

Convicted dumb.

The Red Renault

Maybe to embarrass us, but more so out of economic necessity, our au pair Louise was given a banger to drive me and the sis to school. The older brother, had the car for two years and had run it ragged, by the time we were getting in on the winter mornings, there was a gaper in the floor and you had to slither in between the seized seats to register on the back seats which were grey and stained by life.

It was the bane of my existence. The exhaust was the main source of perpetual shame, it leaked noise in abundance, and Louise would rev it up just for kicks. A 200 metre radius was its range and anyone within this distance had to turn their head in disgust (or so my 10 year old head thought) at our little red ridinghood of poverty. This was complete ridiculousness but in the schoolground it mattered. Louise would drop us off at the launchpad for St Fintans School, "please, wait till we are inside to drive off, please Louise!" she would appease us some days but she held out for the occassion to really throw it at us.

The lineout was jammers, and we were right in the middle, we got out, faces hidden in our armpits, instead of waiting...she drove off slowly alongside us and repetitidly beeped the horn which amalgamated with the burst exhaust and made a toxic noise turning me as angry as my puny body could get, I was horrified, but it was all in my head, nobody ever said anything about it to me, I was just vain and without reason.

Ahhh the trauma of being inside a kids head.

Marbles

School, being inundated with phads, gave marbles a good while. Two years on guesstimate. The game encompassed all the attributes that a kid would like to bring into a brandable personality. You had to incorporate speed tongue, fine motor skills, finesse, bargaining power and dominance upon your siblings. These characteristics floughted there way in through the format of battle.

Firstly you chose your opponent, usually the one with marbles that you would like to acquire. Bum bags around your waist, you pulled out your roller and matched it against the flavour your opponent pulled out. Bargaining branched. If your marble was better you got odds such as twoesy-onesy or if yours was way better you got threesy-onesy. This ramified that he had to knock yours thrice for him to win, while you only had to hit his once. Whence both parties were appeased or pushed into battle by the crowd, you let the onesy marble pick the spot to start from.

Now came the speaksies. He threw his marble and you began an onslaught of phrases which he had to deflect for you not to be allowed one of the best options for your initial go.

He threw and so began the barrage; "no dropsies(walking straight up to the opponents marble to where he dropped his marble from a vertical position, resulting in imminent destruction) no rollies (where the opponent was dis-enabled the advantageous position of rolling their marble along the floor which was particularly dangerous in cornered areas where rebounds were inevitable) no flukesies (stopped the opponent walking up to whatever position suited them best, as long as you were a metre away)."

If you got these three would be hazardous phrases out before your opponent could, he only could get kicksies(self explanatory) lobsies(where you had to overarm marble chuck which was danger in the lunchtime courtyard!) or the suckiest of the throws which was underies; an underarm throw which meant you had to judge the bounce which was fierce difficult in the yard, as it was not exactly flat.

Once that process of " I called this...No you didnt," was decided by the crowd and among yourselves, the second throwee played his part, trying to knock his marble off the first marble thrown. If you missed the ranting began again, so you had to be on your toes. If he knocked yours, you started again as long as there was a twoesy-onesy on. This all made perfect sense.

If a few classes of the Sixteen that existed in St Fintans primary school were out on a trip. The yard was emptier which created the environment for cross yard marbles. This brought moments of exemplary motor skills and judgement. The marbles had gas names and one was by far the most provocative, named the spotted dick, it was desired, expensive and colourful. I went in for a sixesy-onesy with a red haired rich kid one day, he had bought the shop of marbles, lonely child syndrome I suspect.

The whole class was watching as I widdled him down to onesy-onesy with rapid fire "dropsies!" and "flukesies," I had him on the rails but break was on its last time legs and games were never brought on to lunch which transpired two hours later(an infinity in kid reality). The lines were beginning to accumulate for the walk into class and everyone felt the bell on the ring. I got an underies and his huge spotted dick was 30 yards across the yard. There was no time for tactics like laying up and hoping he would miss, leaving me with a shorty. There was only one way, a bazooka throw, out from out where! So I belted my little squizzle(small normal coloured spiral marble) into the stratosphere and it came hurtling down on top of his ball just as the bell frung out its sound... The walk in was a triumphant march.

Johnny The Bus Driver

'Dublin Bus' was great. Everyday it would wait outside St Fintans primary school until everylast teenybopper was accounted for. It began at thirty pence a trip which slowly decreased to free with Johnny's soundness correlating in tandem. The school bell was a resounding frequency which allowed about ten minutes to catch the green wheely wonder outside the school.

It was a number 31 and although it was busted beyond any normal bus, it sufficed and exceeded any medium for freedom that we could have imagined. It served mostly Howth and the outer Sutton area. It began with the South hill territory which had the cutist girls and the bentist lads. They were bullies that could not do their job due to Howths overwhelming numbers on the bus. Some randomers hopped at the summit and made their merry way home without friends to kick it along the way with. Casana View pulled in some heads, but only after letting of snotser.

The fella had snot dribbling from his rivernostrils all day long. It must of been a disease or some sort of curse for it was a veracious way to get a kid abused during school. his gaff was always freaky, surrounded with old ships, hedges with holes and boots hangin off the telephone wires. One day, Johnny had to maul the druel monster off the green when he started a scrap with a girl. He must not have liked her functioning nose . We think he brought himself up in that mysterious house.

Johnny would ask how your day was, glasses falling of his face but never on the floor as he had a good long chin equipped for catching. He stuck it out as he asked you questions, twitched his eyes a little and to my knowledge was fairly blind. The same navy trousers wore him everyday and his manner of driving bordered on the live version of 'Post Man Pat'- a happy man, snoozing along his daily run- doing good deeds for kids such as giving them free rides so that we could save up and hit our sugar hizziiiii at the weekend.

Three of us would get of at our stop. One of our dogs would be waiting there, lip hangin off them. There was a rumbunction of play followed by a chat about when footy would be kicking off in the pitch behind my gaff. Fairly general. One day I arrived back and my Swedish nanny was sprawled up against the hallway wall being banged by her gym instructor. I said I'd walk the block with the lads and not tell them the buzz. Coming back a half hour later my 12 year old eyes got re-stung, she went scarlet and covered herself running off and Pete followed by, kinda half explaining as I walked in the door with a key turn. It looked good too, bet they and there orgasm were pissed at me.

Tweens

Sleepovers

Having spent the day jambling around the gaff with your best or newest friend, the logical progression was to spend the night together hanging. It was kept special by the parents, by it not becoming obligatory with a few cry plea's. During the weekend, one or two friends could stay over and birthdays; well you may not want a party just a sleepover!

It was the test to know how you really got on, there was always war tangles, three in the morning "I want to go home's". It was the separation that helped the growth. Sometimes you would be thrown in with strangers of kids your mom just made friends with and that was a scenario... dark houses, dark moments and inhibitions, grabbing onto your mothers leg as she left and then grabbing reality checkpoint, you would just get on with it! Computer games were a peace medium as were sweets, swings and if you were lucky a beach for a back garden.

One birthday we got to use the lounge for a sleepover which at the time meant I was coming of age, as a rule had been swept aside. A load of local lads arrived and George, a younger fella buzzed over from the Southside, who I had a great time with that summer at soccer camp, but he was younger and easy pickings for the lads.

It all started whimsy with helium balloons and voice contests, choco overload and making songs on the piano we couldn't touch, we watched a Sandra bullock film which started a whole line of who had done what or more like who could bullshit best. There was always some torture masochism when Ciaran the eldest of us was around, ice cubes and boxers I remember followed by the loser sucking on some concoction that no iron stomach could slurp on.

Sleep began to creep and the real shit started going down, as going asleep first on a sleepover was a no-go… maybe sleepovers on the Southside were more refined but George couldn't cope with the no sleep dealio and without acknowledgement; George was covered in sauces, soap in hair, matches in mouth and wet all over his boxers being awoken to tell him of his accident. Eyelids with jam and with tiredness slipping him in and out of consciousness it must have been a nightmare. We all got a bit of that, as staying awake was improbable but sleeping was a heavy fine.

We snook out of the house, Ciaran the Pied Piper of mischief and ran across the field to throw stones at a girls house who we all fancied, burning off when her parents woke… legging it back to retrieve bikes, we whirled around the block in the wee hours thinking we owned the place! By morning George was getting grumpy and throwing digs, which was fair enough, mom woke and made croissants with jam which we all fell asleep eating.

Sleepovers; the young hangover.

Rollerblades

Among all the phads the Americans gave us, rollerblades were long termers. Where pogs, bmx'x, skateboards and sticker collecting were richter in there epic rise and fall, rollerblades used all four wheels to keep trendy. They made girls wear skirts and dudes sport jeans made by 'Xworx' which then had to be ritualistically cut and shredded into a shadow of there formal selves. The 'Xworx' logo was of some long haired kid with a spraycan, he was an idol that we all wore with pride.

Distances became trips and boundaries crumbled. A new cycle track on the strand road made town doable and yeah it got grokked! Thormanby was full of kerbs, walls and bushes to flirt with. The concrete was smooth and entire days of blading 'around the block' were as common as bleeding knees. Blading was a justification to throw shapes as well. "dropped your triangle there," you would get told if you were bowling around flamboyantly, but on blades you had style! Arriving into the estate with your friends all watching you was a trip to egoville, but in Howth they wouldnt let you get away with that too easy, and brought you back down with an embarrissing story about how you ate grass once.

Blading made us hang out and tell stories without getting bored. Three or four girls joined the lads most of the time and that got to us creating some tricks. Starting with 180's we hit 360 spins off kerbs and then eventually tried a few grinds and when we looked shit in front of the girlies, we decided to find a steel pole to practice scratching up on. A dumpster(there was so many in Howth with the whole building boom) checked us a rusty pole which we lubed into a finely polished grinding machine. We brought it down to the nether regions of Howth, into Balscadden tennis courts and banjoed ourselves for days trying to dominate the steel. I gave up, Tony and Andy were better at that stability stuff so I kept maxin the speed thing I had going on, and that kept me with a high chin.

As Howth was hilly which includes a summit, we would roll up to where there was no stopper or T-stop in the world that could slow you down. Looking down on the landscape from summit car park is a road that ends in a main road, trees to the left and hefty bushes to the right. We duck toe'd it down!! on one knee, the other leg bent so the toe of your boot balanced you, we would melt down holding hands, covering the road in a five man V. Towards the end, it was every man for himself; most bailed, blemming into kerbs or trees but every once in a while if we felt lucky in the unity, we would cross the road and meet the far kerb, a destiny that seemed a mile away from the top of the sprint.

There was a computer game on the 'Sega Megadrive' at the time called 'Skitchin' which is kind of self explanatory. Emulation was the only fruit to be picked. On another smooth road away from the summit towards the estate, we would huddle into a group, slowing down cars and then ask the driver some mundane question; giving the skitcher time to grab onto the back. Then we would all grok as the unknown passenger would trundle down the road into imminent pain. We were better at the Megadrive.

Au Pairs

Mom and Dad were very busy heads. Dad was playing golf Tuesday through Sunday on the tour and Mom was modeling, helping run the family bakery business and being fabulous. To ensure that they and us could survive, we got second parents in the form of Au Pairs from exotic foreign countries like Spain, Sweden and France.

A new person would arrive out from the blue and then we would spend a year or two in their fine company. Most of our Au Pairs were brilliant. We had two memorable disasters. One German dude stayed in the mews across from our gaff and smashed an entire glass table and put the contents into 2 litre coke bottles before skipping off in the middle of the night. Another chick ran out on us after trying to hit me and Chloe when we were down in Cork with the parents out and about. Gas days! Me and chloe went running around the holiday homes looking for other heads and found some saviour.

The old nannies included Anne, the larger than life women from Arklow who had enough humour to fill the house to the rafters. She was a great soul and taught us a lot about living. There was Lina the blond soccer player from Sweden who taught us to cook and played fuzzball with me which garnered huge kudos from the footy lads. At this stage we were well into our Swedish au pairs and so came Christina, who was gas craic. Mad moxy, red hair and was out and about a lot. She shared a lot of wisdom and thrust the transition of teenage on me and Chloe. When she left there was serious pains as she was a cool older friend in the house.

Lastly, Sofia came and made a huge impact. Me and Chloe adored her and we learned a lot about Swedish culture, cooking pancakes and smorgosborg Christmas's. Mom died around the same time as Sofia arrived and as Sofia got on so well with me and Chloe and she was very beautiful, my Dad and her eventually came together and have been married for ten years and have two new children. In the end our au pairs really did become part of the family.

Golf Ball Hunting

Golf was an integral part of the childhood. Dad was a professional and everybody else around him rejected the game. So out came me and I became a possibility. Each sunday me and chloe were treated to maccy D's after an hour in the driving range. Golden arches are bribery. Interest grew and I got a set of clubs that pushed the idea of playing. As a course lied nearby, whoever I could find would come along and we would sneak onto 'Deer Park' par three course and play but more so, take chunks out of the course.

We lost so many fricking golf balls, as there was gorse bush everywhere! Business opportunities come from struggle though. As we got ripped by the brambles, thorns and birds claws, our pockets began being filled with golf balls! way more than we even lost. Some fella saw us come out of no mans land one day and asked us if we had any balls for sale. We were taken aback but had plenty of rubber for sale. He offered us an Irish punt for three balls! now that was a lot of sweets or premiership stickers which were the craze at the time. We spent the rest of the day hanging out in the brush, and wandering around bad golfers ever-ready to pop out and give them the speele.

We learned the haggle, the way of old men and to laugh when comments were not funny. I had an old english red telephone box for the savings, it rattled for two years until girls grew breasts.

Truth N Dare

Downing mischief is an impossible task. The amount of troublesome
ideas a "young one" had were myriad. One way to get all the
underlying jest out of ourselves, was to loosely play a truth or dare
game which made itself up as we went along. Somedays it would take
the form of actions, where we would just dare eachother to
outrageousness, knocking on heads doors and leggin it away, singing
carols to people during the summer, making a fire... to going into the
crazy ladies garden by which we were certain there was no return.

Most of the time it was questions; piercing questions that you could
not get away from. I was asked one day what a 'rainbow kiss' was, I
would not answer in front of the group because I did not know shit
about it. I brought my confidente into the shed outside the gaff and I
told him that it was when you kissed but there was layers in this kiss
which brought more kissing(thinking of it now, its quite poetic) then
all I heard was uproar outside the shed where the whole group broke
themselves laughing at my 'immaturity'. Innocence was bliss, and
torture. A rainbow kiss I later found out was when something
unutterable happens.

We would tell eachother all sorts of skeletons. Had you ever shit
yourself, did you fancy this person had you ever had a wet
dream....what was the strangest thing you have eaten, did you love any
of your teachers, had you kissed a dog and whatever there was in
between.

It was an endless drama, a battle to keep cool and try and act relaxed about the outcome. I was a loser when it came to lying or bullshitting. They would ask and either get the correct embarrassing answer or be told a story so out there that it could not possibly grasp onto any kind of reality checkpoint. The crash and burn scenarios were frequent, the worst I can recollect involves a kissing game that was so base its just plain gas.

We would play truth or dare with three or more of us, usually two guys and Barbera, the girl who had us all under her spell and leash. We would dare eachother to kiss Barbera and it would go down. So one summer juicebox of a 24, we were in my old abondoned garage with nothing but a punch bag and some graffiti, legacies from my brother. We sat up top in some romantic alcove. I had only kissed once before and was not the most proficient. It was me and my two best friends at the time, Ed and Noel and of course Barbera. The two lads had each got a couple of smooches by now and I was very ready, or so I thought I was. Barbera did not want to kiss me but the rules were gonna make her, but she made the rules... I opened my mouth like a fish and closed my eyes waiting for contact... yeah, thats what she did, she spat a nice flemmer into my gob and I spluttered!! the lads dropped it into belly laugh and I got up and ran off, disgusted.

I later got her back three years later when she kinda liked me. It was in the local shed, she asked for a kiss so I sat down beside with the tact of a porn star and waited for her to peal her lips which I then against every good bone in my body, performed the retribution deed and laughed with the occupancy of the shed. She did not understand at first why I did it, but she caught the jist in the end

GAA Discos

Cold cold mornings. Saturdays many of them, were spent at the Gaelic football club beating and being beaten by some other locality of kids within Dublin. Barr was the main joker, "ref! hes hanging out of me like a monkey!!" he would say as some fella mauled him in the air. It was good crack but I secretly wanted to be the goalie and so I quit without really explaining why and then joined the football team to become a shotstopper.

The Gaa club building was a dingehole of a place. It had copious amounts of Coco Cola and crisps which made everything alright. There was four booths filled with mangey couches and then some wooden tables and chairs. The dj spun cheese in the corner on a little raised platform which was devided from the "dancefloor" that was a triangle area of grey plastic flooring. The curtains were always closed and it was a sweatbox! but it was Howths sweatbox and it was the greatest thing since Nintendo.

It was where I got abused for dancing like a chicken and kissing like a fish. Randomers would approach you " will ya meet me mate" pointing at some timid creature in the corner. When a girl came up and asked for a dance herself you were in for it. You would grapple onto the waist and see how it went, scared shitless of stepping on toes or falling over.

Sometimes you got your hole and kissing was the closest thing to sweets, so many correlations in those times as all emotions got mixed together under the category of "good" I had one girl who really liked me and I kind of regret not treating her better now but I just did not have that vavaboom for her. Patricia was her name and she was my stalker. She sent beautifully hand made Valentines cards and always smothered me with attention when I was around, but being a bloke who knew football as my best friend, I could not deal with that kind of feeling and pretty much ignored her.

We went out for two days, I giving in to friends pressures to give her a chance which ended up in me breaking her heart because I just did not get it. She was my best girl friends cousin and that hurt things bad.

But all was still cool at the disco, I was told that I was to be bashed by her big brother but that blew over and I performed a charity dance with her one night which I remember enjoying because she was a lovely spirit, one that I could not harness in my inadequacies.

There was always at least one domestic going on, some kind of gossip that had been stirred and now a fight was in order to sort it out. I was a puff but knew how to punch and so never got picked on, but that disco must have been hell for some heads. The ramifications of the nights would be whispered around Howth for weeks until the next one, when your cred could be restocked.

Drinking, laughing, fighting and scoring, suppose its still the same in 'grown up' world.

Bailey Jumps

The curtains woke you up, there was no denying them. It was sunny and you were not getting away with it. Some yum yum, on with the rollerblades and a towl in hand, it was beach time alright. It was not really a beach though, more so a contingency of rocks that jutted into perfect verandas.

Getting there was always a gas. We would meet somewhere usually the summit shop,get some cookies for the trip and blem down the hill towards the 'Bailey', at least one of us getting some bloodknees for the adrenaline barter. The alley down to the bailey was a jungle during summer, nettles and buzzards wrecking the cheese. The mud path winded round the headland and out from a rhododendron bush there peered the sea giving us a wink with its shimmer.

Fears mounted no matter how many times you made the trip down. You stood gawking at the jumps from two hundred feet, a betaunted wire fence that held the flimsy yellow sign "dangerous cliffs, do not pass this point." As with all of Howths great finds, somebody had laid a path, in this case a rope as well, which hung down the entire mud face that we all tugged on our way down.

Water scared my little inhibited bones, I rarely jumped, usually just hanging out with the girls destined for a gayness that never came. There was loads of options, for the entrepid there was a gajillion. The 'pussy futter' was about 10 feet high while the ultimate was a double decker bus. The scenarios that flashed when the edge caught your toes were frickin multi! I watched the lads springbox off the ultimate or the tropical(where you jumped off a deranged looking rock) and attempt the carry that made water splash and not flesh crunkle.

One day I conjured enough balls (or ate enough weetabix) to fall off the pussy footer. I came up sputtering, half dead because I belly flopped and in wondrous delight. I still did not do it again for another 5 years.

Somedays we would wander further a field and ahoy Jamesons beach. Here, there was a rock pool but the only really good thing was the girls did more sun bathing and that meant somebody had to put on the sun tan lotion...

Knacker Drinking

By definition, knacker drinking is the consuming of alcohol outside the usual forums and conventions that convey drinking surroundings. Pubs are fields, alleyways and trees while parties are always of the beach and golf course variety. It was that silly age that made you do it. At 14 to16 you cant get drink in a pub or an offo unless you shaved yourself too young as a lad and were already growing a wolf face. I was a smooth criminal in the chin department and took up the occupation of a weekly beg by the offo. It would be Friday at 7 o'clock and we would be creeping round Howth village looking shady. If one of our brothers friends or anybody who looked like a compassionate sort (for everybody understands in Ireland how important a drink is) then we would grab some courage and drop the line. " Will you go into the offo for us?" they would either light up, knowing that older ones had done this for them as a teenager, or get on their moral horse and ride the selfish track.

We always got lucky; most felt it was their obligation to let us see the world through beer goggles. Some would not get vodka, just beer and other non-hospitalising substances. When they said they would do the deed, the adrenaline began pumping and when they strode out with a blue plastic bag, we all nearly wet our pants with anticipation. As we got older we tried ourselves. For this there were set rules, the rest of

the crowd had to be undetectable in the village so that
if the offo manager came out the fella who was trying to get served
was not stung with buying for under-agers, wrecking the night for all
of us. Mick grew up fast and could get the job done at 15. A night on
which a friend had a free yacht in Malahide was an occasion. Mick
launched up to the main street off licence and bopped in the red doors.
The four of us were huddled down the road 40 yards, scenarios of
drunkenness flickering through the brain. He walks out with his hands
full and the delight is huge within the group. We stalk over to him
when out props the manager! Seeing the buzz he shouts… " You're
barred... for life!!" but he lets us keep the drink and we don't live in
Malahide. Good times.

Making a mixer in your house on the sly was a formidable option. It
was risky but the concoction always got you in a hoop! There was a
tent full of girls in Catherines house one summers night and the lads
had set up intentions to wander on down there when darkness fell.
About six of us were sleeping over in my gaff and everything was
going to scale as we snook out at 12 that night, plastic bottles of
cocktails that included so many ingredients that the mixture had
curdled.

There was a short cut down to Catherine's through a nettle field, over
a stagnant river trickle and up the trammers... Fields lay on either side
of the trammers...We got down to a sitting spot, which was also great
for rallying around on a bike as there were some minny ramps.

We ploughed ourselves there and popped the lids of our home brew. It was vile. It had whisky, port, baileys, peach juice and orange juice topped of with cointreau. After my fourth gulp I was struggling while the rest of the lads seemed to be gladness personified.

It happened, I took a huge gulp as we were playing a drinking game and wanted to look hard and out it came in reverse like a hose regurgitating some peachmilk. It kept coming until there was a river, out the nostrils and all. The girls arrived up to get us, it did not put Nicole off for I scored that night, and I must have tasted repugnant.

Virginity

By the mid teens it was all kicking off. Girls were different now and so were we. When they were around there was an edge to everything. Words became misconstrued and all of a sudden a walk became an erotic rendez-vous. It was all insecurities about your man hood, periods and bases. Some lads had beards already while most were in envy and could only vouch that they had pubic hair. It was also the time of our first big exams and that made everything more important. The junior cert took second place to the female.

A Danish girl had been in my class for two years and I had never even looked at her, that is until she had boobs. She was clever and I was a messer. In third year, she wore tight jeans and cut her hair short, from a 'I hate my parents hairstyle' to a 'I wanna be your lover' scandinavian style. The first spark is unknown, but I think it shook from the mantle on the hockey pitch. She had a little co-ordination and I loved sports. We were getting somewhere and by Christmas I could not wait for a reason to see her outside school, to gauge what was really going on.

Sarah Janes party was lame, but Stina was there and wearing white like an angel. There was a kiss and my was it public! in the middle of the dance floor as everyone sang to the girl for her birthday, me and Stina broke it down and melted into a teen moment of pure intoxication. There was no words over Christmas, just flutters.

When we got back, there was awkward air but my best mate Steve had scored Stina's best friend Cara and we doubled up for a Saturday in town (who we later called president bush, when one night she got mangled drunk, her jocks fell down and we carried her up the stairs to bed, bush on show). I got kissed, very badly it must be said, she had not much practice and Steve found out that Cara was frigid or timid(which were the same thing back then, as the lads had the feelings of buffalo)

We were coupled and the year ran along with escalating love, until we told eachother in May after an overwhelming smooch on the couch. The exams turned over saying hello to freedom, I got my braces off and Stina had a free gaff! Her decision had been coaxed by an imminent parting that was moving her life to Denmark and mine to England within a month. By the weekend of consummation, we were rosy ready, but of course she needed compassion and understanding when it came to the nightime. We had been watching the Eurovision and now I wanted to make her sing. We went to her cute bedroom and when the moment came to put on a jonny and do what I had been waiting 15 years to do, little Dylan aborted mission on me.

I had gone so flaccid from fear that I might as well of not had one. I was shaking and Stina was now the one coaxing. She was tender and relaxed me and then gave it the juice and revived. All flipped again for she was in pain when we first embraced. Thinking in my teenage nature, the only example of sex I had seen were of men jamming women out of it! So I went and had the only sex I knew. I thrusted kind of hard and grabbed the bed railings, feeling like I was doing everything right. It was when she was crying that I realised and we slowed into a hug. later that night was much better.

The End

Thanks and more Thanks!

Where does one start! From the foetus to the present... how many words, hands and actions to thank, how do you quantify how one person cares over the other, it is all an accumulation of great movements and moments.

There are not many who believed in this project along with myself... I would like to thank my first and still one of my best friends Ciaran O'Conluain.. He has always brought up these stories with glee and kept plugging away at me to do something with them. Ever Since I was lucky enough to meet my magical partner Rani, she has had a huge impact on the project, having helped with initial edits and more recently with layout, design and most importantly, offering unconditional encouragement and lots of tender love.

To Nigel Linden, who is a superstar! He produced the audiobook version of the stories as a favour and really ignited the move towards publishing the book. My best friend David Quinn who recently got so excited by the book that he re-invigorated the process and for all the chats that went into the edit.

I would like to thank my family, not for any direct part in this book but more for being my family. They are a mad bunch that are far from perfect, but they have given me great inspiration through the struggles as well as good times.

The heads in Howth! What a bunch of characters eminating gas and banter from every pore. From the Thormanby heads extending down to what later became the village heads, I would like to thank Lorna, Dave, Mick and James in particular for some great times and memories.

You cannot really thank a place but if you could I would like to give a warm thanks to Howth inc. For being a true vortex unto itself and an island(it being a peninsula) with all the right stuff and plenty of hardship to help a young one grow up alright.

Dylictionary & Dublinisms!

Frajilistic | brilliant, fantastical

Mahussive | huge! Massive with umph

Fantasmical | play on Fantastic

Shimmeration | shimmer plus plus

The ying yang | a deep somewhere

Madyoke | somebody has a screw loose or ate too many eggs

Fuzzball | soccer/football

Wiseacre | Americanism created by Tom Wolfe

Whimsy | on the edge of whimsical

Young one | an incalcuble age between 8 and 26

Shotstopper | goalkeeper in soccer

Grok & Grokked! | excited, overjoy, stoked, yes!! (Tom Wolfe)

Reality checkpoint | a checkpoint on the path

Jist | understand, comprehend the suss

Banjoed | destroyed, wrecked

Gaff | house in Dublinish Slack Alley

 | Alan Partridge term for bad form or actions

Wrecking the cheese | annoying ones brain

Gajillion | many, many, many

Offo | off licence, liquor store

On the sly | without somebody knowing what your up to

In a hoop | destroyed, drunken mess

To scale | as planned

Eurovision| terrible annual European musical talent show

Jonny| condom

www.ingramcontent.com/pod-product-compliance
Lightning Source LLC
LaVergne TN
LVHW041202080426
835511LV00006B/711